MW00803362

Searching for Fred

A True Story

Nava Chernoff

Edited by Alyson Stephan

Searching for Fred
A True Story

ISBN 9781480172821

Dad, I miss you.

Table of Contents

ACKNOWLEDGMENT

I would like to express my deepest and sincerest gratitude to all of the people who have helped and supported me while researching and writing this book. To Tom, my loving husband, whose endless excitement kept me motivated. To my family, who shared vital information throughout my search. To my friends Kelly and Meir, who patiently read every version of this book as it developed into what you are reading today. To the Peeters' and Roni, for being my biggest cheerleaders. To Mom Ora and Mom Alice for always being there for me. To Ms. Kruger--without you, the Youth Trip to Germany would not have been possible. And last, but not least, a very special thanks to my editor and friend, Alyson Stephan, for her countless hours of gentle instruction and guidance.

Preface

This is a true story of an ordinary girl with extraordinary determination.

On his deathbed, Nava's father asked her to find his two brothers and a sister she never knew existed. He explained that they were lost in Europe during the Holocaust, but he wasn't sure of their surnames, as his own had been changed as a young boy.

Nava Chernoff was born and raised in Eilat, Israel's southernmost city located at the northern tip of the Red Sea. At the age of twelve, she decided to leave home to live and work on Kibbutz Maale Hachamisha. When Nava was twenty-five, she began her decade long journey to find her missing relatives.

Now a happily married mother of two, Nava had a tumultuous childhood and a painful divorce. She suffered the loss of her beloved father and stood at her mother's side when she had near-fatal lung cancer. Throughout all of her trials and tribulations, she never gave up on the search to find her lost family.

Chapter 1

Early Childhood

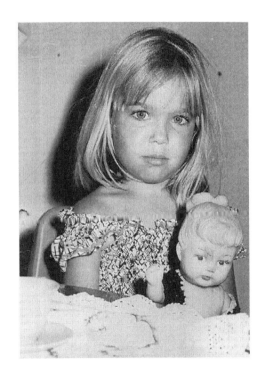

Every little girl should have a dream—a big dream.

I was always fascinated by the Red Sea—its calming, clear blue water, the coral reefs, colorful creatures, and the ecosystem. The more I learned from my parents to respect the Red Sea and the life in it, the more I loved it.

Growing up vacationing in Sinai, the neighborhood children always compared notes regarding their sea-faring activities. Some people vividly remember their first experience with swimming. Not me. I could never remember when I had learned to swim, or, as my father would phrase it, "learned to float." He would tell me, "You did not swim at first, but you knew how not to drown." He also claimed, "We threw you off the boat, and you floated." My mother smiled at that story. "It was a little extreme, but you were a very young toddler," she said. One thing from my childhood that I remember very clearly is the first time I swam with a shark. I was five years old. There was an odd, tickling movement around my feet as I stood in the shallow water, looking to the horizon with admiring eyes as my father sailed away on his little fishing boat to catch some fish for dinner. The water was clear and the sand soft. Looking down to see what kind of fish was so playful, I saw it—almost flat, swimming at the bottom around me, brushing my feet.

"Shark!" I shouted as loud as I could. "Shark!"

While in the water, I tried to lift both of my legs up so that the shark could not bite me. My older brother thought this was a funny sight and laughed so hard he was having trouble breathing. My younger brother inched toward me so slowly that a sea turtle walking on the sand would have beat him in this race to save my life.

When Arye finally got to me, I clung to his neck, choking him, my legs around his hips, certain that I would be this shark's dinner. I was scared to death, and I told myself I would never, ever go back into the sea. As I looked at the beautiful blue water from afar, I immediately regretted my thoughts. My mother did everything in her power to convince me that—from the description my brother gave—it was a sand shark and they were harmless. My brave, larger-than-life father came back from fishing to hear my two older brothers laughing as they told him about the incident. My father's words were so calming and reassuring when I received my first lesson about sharks.

"Sand sharks will not harm you," my father said.

"This is what Mom told me, too," I replied, not quite convinced by this theory. There was no way that I was going to believe him. Not on that day. I opened my eyes as big as I could—they are big and green just like my Dad's eyes—and I answered back, "It was going to eat me! It touched my feet. It wanted my feet first." There he went again, my brother Elan, laughing so hard—until he got The Look from my Dad. "It will not eat you and now you will go back to the sea and swim with us," Dad said. Elan was thirteen years old and Arye was twelve years old. They ran into the water with my tall, slender mother (who was very active and often swam with us), but I stood still. I said, "Not me! I am not going!" I was such a stubborn little girl.

Dad picked me up. "Back to the water you go," he said. "No shark will eat my daughter today."

I was hoping Mother would come to my rescue, but this time she was clearly on Dad's side.

"You should go into the water and swim," she said. "Learn about its creatures so you will not be afraid."

My parents had lost it, for sure. Here I was, five years old, almost attacked by a shark and my Dad and Mom were going to throw me back into the ocean. I could not admit to my parents that day—as I made quite a fuss over the sand shark—that, after I was dropped back into the water and looked down to see it, the sand shark was pretty cute.

I have learned many lessons regarding the sea; the list grows longer as I get older, and yes, I learned that sand sharks will not eat me. We spent every holiday on the beach, playing in the soft white sand of Sinai, Mother running the show and Father out there fishing. On one of those holidays, I ended up in Yoseftal hospital in Eilat. We gathered all the equipment—which included our swim gear, toys, coolers, clothes, tents, garbage, etcetera—and we were missing a cup from the new red set of dishes. We all searched for it. Dad cleaned the grill and for the first time, and last ever. He poured the hot charcoals on the sand. During the search, I stepped on the hot charcoals. As a reflex, I lifted my leg up, putting my second foot on the charcoal. With burning feet, I ran into the Red Sea. My thoughts of going back to the others to tell them what happened abruptly ended when I realized how badly I was burned and how painful the hot, dry sand was. I would have to stay in the water until someone came to my rescue.

"What is wrong?" my mother asked. "It is not like you not to help."

I told her what had happened and showed her my feet. My mother's deep brown eyes looked worried and sad as she smiled and assured me that I would be fine as soon as they got me to the hospital. Dad carried me to the Jeep. The search for the cup ended abruptly as the ride to the hospital began. While we were in the car, I started to feel blistering on the bottom of my feet and I remember thinking that by the time we reached the hospital I would not have any skin at all on my feet. I was too afraid to look, and I had no clue what was happening. Dad was so upset over what happened that when Mom checked on me every few minutes I said I was fine, even though I wasn't. The drive was 75 km (about 46 miles) from Nuwiba, Sinai to Eilat. There were no highways, and the Jeep was far from new. The pain was intense and tears fell down my cheeks even though I tried not to cry. Normally, we would be singing songs the whole way back home. Of course, having four children together in the small space of the Jeep's back seat, there would often be fighting and arguing, but that day we drove back in complete silence. Wrapped up with bandages on my feet, traveling on piggyback for a few days, and listening to the adults cursing about that cup was no fun.

Those adventures on the smooth, sandy beach and in the warm, clear water were endless. We had lots of laughs, too. The story that I heard the most, which happened before I was born, was about one of the trips to Sinai. My parents and most of my siblings left the tent, leaving Ofra, my older sister, to watch it. Ofra had a visitor—a lonely, lost camel. She was so scared of him that she fed him to keep him busy. By the time our parents returned, all of their food was gone.

When I was eight years old, Israel returned our part of Sinai to the Egyptians. Withdrawal from Sinai followed the Israel-Egypt peace treaty of 1980-1982. Dad quit his job and vowed to "never touch Sinai as long as it is under the Egyptians." Mom was not too happy with the fact that Dad needed to look for new job, but it was all for peace. The children of the house quickly learned not to ask to go to Sinai. "You cannot go there anymore," Dad would reply angrily.

After the peace treaty, Dad did exactly what he said he would—he never touched Egyptian soil. I never visited Sinai beaches after the peace treaty, but I visited Egypt in 1992. I found the culture of Egypt rich and fascinating—nothing at all like the stories I heard as a young girl from my father, who was angered by the political situation in Sinai. Maybe one day I will gather enough positive energy to take my children to the beautiful white sand and clear blue water of "RAS GOLDA" in Sinai.

Les Brown—a famous composer and big band leader—said, "Shoot for the moon. Even if you miss, you'll land among the stars."

Pittsburgh, Pennsylvania is 6057 miles from Eilat, Israel, and yet, I can assure you that I did shoot for the moon and landed on a star.

As a mother of two children, I'm always worrying. Are they safe? Did their friends' parents give them something to drink? Did they eat? Will they remember not to play with fire and not to talk to strangers? With all the frightening things going on with the Internet, do you check their computer occasionally? Check their cell phones? The list is a mile long. During every stage of their upbringing, we made it through one challenge just to arrive face-to-face with a new one.

In 1974, my mother was very busy running the house and taking care of all the children—seven all together, and not all her biological kids, but she treated every one as her own. She did the best she could with her situation, married to my father. He was a tough man. He raised the family and worked full time. We lived in a 60 square meter house, which is equivalent to 645 square feet. Of seven children, the youngest was a newborn and the eldest twenty years old. Five of us kids were still living in the house, as my two older sisters were married and living in their own homes. Mother was only twenty-seven years old at this time. How did she do it? I can't even imagine, and things only got more difficult for her in the following years. Having said that, she could not possibly be in one hundred percent control.

I was six years old. He told me he would take me for a walk in the mountains and we would buy a Popsicle on the way back home. I had no reason whatsoever not to believe him—he was part of the family and would never hurt a little girl, especially not me. Off we went for a walk, to the desert mountain that I loved to play on, and he knew it. In a place where no one could see, he told me,

"Turn around and lean on the mountain so I will not see your face."

I was worried because he sounded different than usual. Even his smell changed all of a sudden, but I did what he asked me to. I turned, bracing my hands against the mountain and moving the gravel beneath my feet. I asked him why we can't play facing each other, and he said because this was a big kid's game. Then he rubbed himself on me. I wanted to turn, but he didn't let me. He did this while I was fully dressed and not looking. He made strange grunting noises, and this is when I felt that it must be wrong for him to play with me like that. I was too afraid to make a sound. Finally he said,

"I am done. Let's go back."

I wanted to climb up the mountain and play in the bunker, but he said that we had to go back home so my mother would not worry, and we did. We went back home. I was confused but was not sure what to make of it. Every time he was with me, his advances became more aggressive—to the point that he forced himself on top of me, looking into my eyes while he raped me. I knew then that what he was doing to me was wrong, but I wasn't sure why, except that he was hurting me, and that could not be right. No one else treated me this way. My father was not the most affectionate person, but I knew he loved me and would never hurt me. This child rapist said, "Don't tell anyone," with a combination of fear, pleasure, and anger in his eyes. I was scared, very scared. The pain drove me to find a way to end the assaults. Without telling anyone, I made up my mind that his actions were wrong and I needed to find a way out. I came up with the idea to be with someone at all times, to avoid being alone—no matter what. Today, this is called the "buddy system." It worked for a while, until the holidays, when we had a house full of guests and he stayed the night in our room, the children's room. He slept next to me. When everyone else fell asleep, I could not sleep because I was so frightened that I could not relax. I knew what he was going to do to me. I was worried that if someone saw us like that they would blame me for doing something wrong and throw me out of the house. That was what he told me would happen once, after he raped me. My six-year-old brain was utterly tormented. I remember thinking, "Why is he so afraid that my parents will find out?" So I decided to tell my parents what he was doing, and hope that it would make him stop. When he made advances on me that night, I turned to him and looked at him straight in the eyes; I wanted him to see me in the dark. Then I said, "If you touch me again, I will tell Dad." He looked at me as if he saw a ghost; in an instant he lost his color and started to sweat. It worked. He never touched me again. At six years old, I learned a harsh but important lesson: Words can kill.

Among my friends and family, it is well known; they all say it the same way: "If you do not want to hear the truth, do not ask Nava." I was eighteen when I told my Mother what had happened twelve years earlier. I felt so bad for her. She couldn't believe her ears and could never understand how this terrible thing could have happened in a house so loving, supportive, and open. Why had I not said anything? I did not know what to say to her, knowing she did everything possible to raise us in a positive environment.

My husband and I constantly say to our children, "You are better off telling us what you have done wrong, even though it is bad or you think it's bad, than to have us find out for ourselves," in a way that they know we are not the enemy. We are here to protect, guide, and help them. I was a victim of rape. Did that experience leave a scar on me? Absolutely. I had not been bothered by my past for years; it did not disappear, it was just put to sleep for a while— until our daughter Shani was born, that is. I did not let her leave my sight unless I knew exactly where she was. I did not hold her at home or stop her from going out to play; she was in a daycare while I worked. I could see her through the window when they played in the back yard; the fact that I knew where she was helped me. I don't think anyone around us ever could tell that I was under a watch and it is possible that all mothers watch their daughters the same way I do; I don't know any other way. Shani and Yarden, our son, never heard about this dark past of mine. Now that they are teenagers, we let them walk in the mall without us, but we are still present in the mall, just not physically with them. The first time we said, "Fine, you go. We will meet in two hours.

" Yarden responded with, "Yes! Finally!"

My second sentence was, "Do not take your eyes off your sister."

These adventures, good and bad, made me who I am. I believe that I was born with some of my character, which definitely helped me to be so independent at a young age; it was part of me. Growing up in a lower class neighborhood in Israel made me stronger. We were all the same; we did not know any different. Our toys were the outdoors. The house was for eating and sleeping, nothing else. Our house was so small we couldn't all play in there if we wanted to. There were only two small bedrooms, a tiny kitchen, and a combination living/dining room with a yellow dining table with matching chairs. At some point, my father extended the entry to make another master bedroom, which was just big enough for two dressers and a double bed. The kid's rooms each had four storage drawers with mattresses inside that rolled out and Mom would have to make every bed each night. All the neighborhood kids played together—old and young. Our soccer ball was patched and stitched so many times that it was no longer round. I was so happy when my sister grew out of her skates and gave them to me. Mattel made them, and they had two straps: one in the front to tie over the toes and one to tie around the ankle. The straps were red leather and so stretched that they looked like they were going to tear. The four wheels on each were worn down to nothing, the ball bearings were filled with sand, and when I tried to skate in them, I barely moved. But I was happy and proud because they were mine. We walked to the abandoned bunkers in the mountains to play, and we loved it. By the time we got back home, we were hungry and tired, and our parents had no problem getting us to sleep.

My first bicycle was so beautiful. I loved it. I received it as a present for my ninth birthday. It was bright red, but it needed some cosmetic touch-ups. It had a frame and two wheels, and not much more. It was my favorite mode of transportation for years to come. My parents got divorced when I was seven years old. One of their biggest problems was that they did not agree on how to raise us children in the house. Dad was tough. I had a completely different relationship with him than my brothers and sisters did. Their memories are not even close to my "rose-colored" life. Somehow, I knew how to get to his heart. Dad was like a coconut stuffed with creamy chocolate—he was hard nut to crack, but if you could, he was soft and sweet forever. Not many people had the privilege of reaching the gooey inside of my father. My niece was second and Yarden, our son, was the third—and of course, my mother, whom my father adored.

Food was a big issue constantly under discussion in our house. Dad often berated my older siblings, and finally Mom could not take it anymore. In one explosive argument, Dad said, "There's the gate! There's a door! You can leave!"

He regretted those words until the day he died. I came home from school and found the glass on my parents' bedroom door broken. Mom was upset, and Iris, my sister, was crying. I was so confused. I could not remember my Mom ever crying before that day. Mom asked me to get Ofer, my younger brother, from kindergarten. She packed some clothes, all of our school supplies, and left Dad alone. My father was not violent and he never hit us. That day, he was so angry he hit the glass door and smashed it.

For a few weeks, we traveled from a friend's house to a little apartment next to Dad. At the end of the school year, when I was nine years old and in third grade, we moved to a different area of Eilat. At first, it seemed like it was so far from my Dad that I hated Mom for moving us. Mom was good; she let Dad visit us any time he wanted. We could go to visit him any time, and stayed with him on weekends. She did this mostly for me; I was close to my father and struggled with the separation, the divorce, and the move. When I saw the bicycle for the first time in my bedroom at Dad's house, my heart was pounding and my smile grew bigger as I jumped up and down while clapping my hands. I looked at it like it was made of solid chocolate. Do you know what this means? No more buses! I can ride here anytime I want. And I did, riding the bike from one parent to the other for years.

At twelve years old, I was at the sea or riding horses in the desert every spare moment. We had no cell phones. Our parents were definitely not chauffeuring us around town. Getting back from school happened by foot or by bus if we were lucky. When I arrived home after school, I would make a sandwich and leave a note on the table that read:

```
Mom,
I am fine, school was good.
Down at the beach, maybe at Texas.
Don't worry, will be back before dark.
Love,
Nava
```

Can you imagine? If I were to come home to find a note like that on the kitchen table, our kids would not be happy campers when they returned, and they had better be home before dark.

I was a good girl, very trustworthy and honest, never got into trouble, and I did not do drugs. However, my grades dropped and school became a burden. I used to love school, but now I wanted to be somewhere else. The Red Sea was calling me— the water, the sea breeze whistling my name and the sun waiting to cover me with a soft warm blanket while on a horse.

Back to the note on the kitchen table...at first, I added a date to my notes, but after a while I stopped. I could use the same note. Only another mother can recognize my Mother's frustration and fear with that "don't worry" note of mine. It did not take long for me to see that I was headed in the wrong direction and needed help to get back on track. I told my parents that I was leaving home and moving to a Kibbutz. "No, you are not!" They said. I gave them all the right reasons to send me away. I dropped my grades, daydreamed in class about the sea and boys, but nothing helped. They said no. I made up my mind that the only thing for me to do, in order to have good future, was to leave the place I loved most: Home.

In September 1985, I found myself in Kibbutz Maale Hachamisha, next to Jerusalem. It was exactly the opposite of what I had known until then.

Eilat was surrounded by magnificent desert mountains and had the most beautiful sea. In Eilat, I went everywhere by foot. The kibbutz was on a green mountain far from the sea. I found a home away from home. I was "adopted" by many kind and patient adults who raised and guided me in the kibbutz. I felt assured and also like a very fortunate young lady. The Ron family was first and then the Nitzan family. Avi and Erit did everything possible, with much success, to make me feel secure around them. I was loved and guided by them. In difficult times, Badana's hot chocolate was a great comfort. When I couldn't reach my mother at home in Eilat for our debates, Sarah was my refuge. It took me longer than I had anticipated, but my grades looked better with help from Meir W. Later, when I became a new mother, Shoshi and Arlene were there for me any time, day or night. I became good friends with the local teens. Among my good friends was Hagar. We spent so much time together. Miriam and Moshe, Hagar's parents, took me in under their wings, too. Moshe was running the stables and spent endless hours with me. Most of the lessons were good. Some were tough, because there were no shortcuts and no discounts. The work needed to be done exactly as he said. It was not easy for someone like me, with my own thoughts and ideas, but there was no way to argue with Moshe; I would lose no matter what. The horses were his domain. If I wanted to be around these majestic animals, I had to listen and obey—no ifs, ands, buts, or maybes. I was fourteen years old when the true meaning of the word "guilt" came into my reality for the first time in my life. It all happened after I was asked by Moshe to feed the horses at dinnertime. I was "busy" with my friends and I did not feed the horses. I did not feel great about it but did not think much of it, either. Depending on your teachers and guides—and your own moral compass—you will learn from your mistakes. I couldn't lie to Moshe when I was asked if I had fed the horses. He gave me such a speech and made sure I understood it the first time. He told me to go back to my dorm—he needed no more help from me. I had betrayed the one person who trusted me. It was guilt indeed. After that incident, Moshe knew it would never happen again, and he was right.

For twelve years, I worked with Moshe in the stables. He treated me like he treated his son. Many times he was my shoulder to cry on or the one to ask for advice. I loved and respected Moshe like a father. I came to realize that I was a nature girl. I loved the kibbutz. I lived there for fifteen years. My children were born there.

Chapter 2

Teenage Know-It-All

The challenges of the teen years are much greater than what the teenager himself thinks while he is passing through them. He says things like, "I know," "Yes, I know," "Don't tell me, I know." I heard these three sentences so many times a day that I found myself telling our son,

"I know you know, but..."

One day, he replied, "I am going to believe that you know."

Often I wonder if the "I know" comes from defending their inner turmoil.

I did not have the privilege of saying, "I know." I clung to what I really knew and learned what I did not know. What other choice did I have? None.

Over the weeks, Moshe and I planned when and where we would ride. By doing so, we could tell someone at home—usually Moshe's wife Miriam and my roommate Noa—when we would be back. It was a safety issue, which was important since we had no mobile phones then. It was a beautiful spring day. The air so fresh after the rain, birds singing, flowers blooming, and calmness in the surroundings made it the perfect weather for a long horseback ride. That had not been in our plans, but we could not resist the invitation by nature. We called Miriam and told her that we were going on a longer trip. We packed sandwiches, fruit, a fingan for field coffee, and all the equipment we needed for an all-day ride. Moshe saddled Sivan and I decided to ride on Rimi; she was an easy ride, especially for the long ones. We had just left the stable and had not even ridden around the curve, when Rimi saw something crawling fast on the dirt between her hoofs and went crazy. She reared up on her back legs and made frantic noises— a high-pitched steady whinnying followed by a lower whimper—over and over again. I was frantic and clung to her neck, afraid to let go. Moshe asked me to take a deep breath and listen to him. "Release the extra rope," he said. After taking a deep breath and listening to Moshe repeating his instructions, I finally did what he asked of me; first, I got control of my fears and then I helped Moshe to help me to gain control of Rimi, my "easy ride." Moshe took hold of the rope and slowly added pressure to Rimi and got control of her. It was the first time that my horse had ever gotten out of control. We all calmed down, including Sivan, Moshe's horse.

Moshe said, "We have two options: one is to go back to the stable and the second is to continue with our plan."

If it had been only me, no doubt I would have gone back. I had a brave face but my heart was pounding fast.

I replied, "Let's continue with our plans; it is a beautiful day." I swallowed hard.

Moshe knew I was pretending—besides the fact that he had two teenage daughters, and the stable attracted plenty of our kind. Although I was sore from the long ride, watching the beautiful sunset made me feel peaceful and calm—feelings I did not have very often. On this beautiful spring day, I had one of the most educational and memorable trips I ever made with Moshe. We talked for hours about fears, senses, control, and horses. When we got back, I was so happy I wanted to hug Moshe and thank him for a great day, but I didn't. After the unpacking, cleaning, feeding, and just before I said good night, Moshe said, "I am so proud of the way you handled yourself today."

I said, "Thank you, see you. Good night," and went to my room with tears in my eyes. Moshe very rarely was fuzzy and warm in the stables, but that evening he acted more like a father than my supervisor.

Noa saw me first, as I entered our room. "Are you okay?" She asked.

"I could not be better," I replied with a smile. "These are happy tears."

I got married despite my father, Moshe, and Avi's disapproval. They did everything in their power to make me understand that getting married was the wrong thing for me to do at that time. I thought I knew better. Avi was a dear friend who lived in America. Cincinnati, Ohio, to be exact. When he came to visit Moshe at the kibbutz, they always went riding together. When I joined them, they loved to torment me. Even to this day, I do not know if I loved it or hated it. Avi was very direct. Whatever was in his mind was on his tongue. He would say, "Do you use drugs? Are you keeping your grades decent? How about safe sex? Do you have any boyfriends?" I kept my answers as short as I could, sometimes with a blush on my cheeks. I would say, "No, yes, none of your business, yes." I would have the most trouble with "none of your business." By the end of our rides, he knew everything, even the "none of your business." Every few months, Avi would get a full report of my life. Moshe said that after my marriage I would visit the stables less often. He was right, as usual. I was still very active in the stables after the marriage, but when I was pregnant with Yarden, I slowed my help. I was seven months pregnant on my last ride. Maybe I would have ridden longer if Doron's surprised gallop while searching for Avi and Sivan hadn't coerced my horse into doing the same. Even though I had no problem slowing her down, I saw Moshe's worried face and in silence we agreed that this would be my last ride for a while. I was back on the horse two months after I gave birth. But now I was a mother, and I made extra precautions to be safe. Before Yarden, I wore a helmet only on long trips. After Yarden's birth, I wore it on every ride. I also made sure to wear boots and checked the saddle twice. My parenting instincts kicked in immediately. I was still active in the stable, and Yarden often came with me. After Shani's birth, I cut my visits to the stable tremendously. I helped Moshe on the weekends with the feeding. Yarden and Shani loved to visit the stable, because right after the feeding I would take them to the petting zoo in the kibbutz. Mostly, I became Moshe's emergency contact. I was there when Moshe needed help with a sick horse or with feeding the horses while he was away.

In September 2008, Avi told me that Moshe had lung cancer. I had high hopes for his speedy recovery, of course. My Mom is a lung cancer survivor. What I did not know there was a "good" cancer until I found out that Moshe had the bad one. He was fighting it in a way that only Moshe could. In September 2009, I realized that the man that I respected so much was living on borrowed time. I talked to Tom, my second spouse, about my feelings and frustrations. I feared that I would never see Moshe again—an impossible, heartbreaking thought. After exhausting our options and with much excitement, we decided that in spite of the bad timing financially, I should fly back to Israel to visit Moshe and say goodbye.

Just before my Dad passed away, there were so many things I wanted to tell him, but I hadn't gotten the chance. I wanted to know why he was so harsh and tough with people, why he couldn't be gentle like he is with my son, Yarden. I wanted to hug him more than just when we said hello and goodbye. I can remember Dad showing emotion five times since I was born. The first, when Mom casually did what he recommended and went thru the door and the gate and never came back. Second, when Dad gave me away at my wedding. Third, when Or, my niece, was born. Fourth, when Yarden was born and Dad had the honor of being his Godfather. Dad had tears coming down his cheeks and his hands were shaking when he held Yarden in the B'rith. I knew then we did the right thing by asking Dad to be Yarden's Godfather. The guests standing around him were worried that Dad would drop Yarden, but I assured them that there is no way dad will let any harm come to Yarden as long as he lives. I was right. The last one; when I came back from Germany with pictures of his baby brother's grave. The rest of the time he was either angry or hiding his emotions, and all I wanted to do was to understand why.

I was determined not to make the same mistake twice, and although with Moshe there were different closures, we still had lots to talk about. I made up my mind to talk to Moshe and tell him what was on my mind, to thank him for the days he taught me and even for the days he was rough to the point that I did not want to see him ever again. I wanted to have a conversation with him once more. Moshe was taller than the average man, but his presence always made him seem larger-than-life. He was well built with salt and pepper hair and strong worker hands, which seemed slightly dirty even when they were clean. He was still working a full schedule, so it was not urgent to fly to Israel immediately. We worked the calendar and booked the trip for October 3rd.

A week before my flight, I received a call from Avi. He asked, "Where are you?"

"I am filling the car with gas."

"Are you okay to talk?"

Avi was never concerned with what position you were in; he would say anything that was on his mind right away, even if it would embarrass you. I felt that he was going to hit me hard.

"Wait," I said. "Let me go in the car." I got in, and said, "I am ready, give me the news."

"Moshe had a blood clot and his mobility was affected. From what I understand it has nothing to do with the cancer, just really bad luck."

Avi did not know all the details yet. I told Avi that I was flying to Israel in a week, and wondered if I should I change my ticket. When I called Tom, he heard in my trembling voice that something was not quite right.

"What is the matter? You do not sound right."

"I am fine but Moshe is not. Can you come home earlier today please?"

When Tom arrived home, we debated whether to change the flight. We had scheduled everything. We had changed Shani's practice hours, had a driver —Kelly M., a dear friend and a neighbor who went out of her way to help—and the school was informed that I would be absent. It looked like Mission Impossible to change the flight and inform everyone of the change. That week seemed to be one of the longest weeks I had ever experienced. By the time I visited Moshe in the hospital, he was refusing just about everything, including food and water. I wanted to do reflexology, but he said no. After a while, one of his visiting friends wanted him to drink. He said no, but when the straw was in his mouth, he drank. It was almost as if we read each other's minds. While Miriam went to the nurse and asked for massage cream, I washed my hands and was ready to massage. The cream was cold; I was afraid Moshe would resist it, so I went back to the sink and warmed my hands in running water, and then did reflexology. I massaged Moshe's feet; he looked like he was enjoying it and showed no resistance. I could not have the conversation I wanted. The situation was wrong; talking to him without him being able to respond was not what I had in mind. Moshe looked at me while I massaged his feet. I felt that he knew I had crossed the ocean just for him.

I came to say good-bye to a man who was a second father to me.

On Thursday, the third day of my visit, I said good-bye, knowing my flight was on Friday and I could not be sure I would have time to visit again. I had promised myself before the visit not to cry, to be strong. I believe in miracles and wanted to hold on to positive thoughts. None of it worked. I was strong facing Moshe, but as I hugged Miriam, the tears just came. I never wanted them, but when they came, they did not stop for long time. Instead of me telling Miriam to be strong and positive she told me,

"I am happy you visited us. Thank you and be strong."

I could not leave. I told Tom on the phone that I was having a hard time saying good-bye, as I knew I would not see Moshe again after this visit. Tom, with all of his understanding, said, "If you think a few more days will help you, then stay."

How could I stay? It would never be easy— today, tomorrow, or next week. Friday, at noon, I visited Moshe again. Miriam looked at me with surprise.

"If I could, I would stay longer," I told her.

"I know," she replied.

I told Moshe, "I am flying back to the United States. I will call home next week and I hope you will answer the phone."

He nodded.

"Moshe," I told him, "I am writing a book and you are big part of the way I turned out. Can I add a chapter about you and the stables?"

This time, he laughed out loud and said, "Yes!"

I kissed him, kissed Miriam and with a heavy heart, left the two of them in the room. I promised myself not to cry again next to Miriam like I did on Thursday. When I turned to the elevator, I could not stop the tears from going down my cheeks. Noa picked me up from the hospital. I was a mess with makeup running down my face and bloodshot eyes, and exhausted but totally unable to sleep. We drove back to the kibbutz in silence. Moshe passed away shortly after my visit. He is greatly missed by his wife, daughters, granddaughters, family, many friends, and me.

If you were to see Noa, my roommate in the youth house, you would think the team that had come to a resolution for us to share a room had no clue what are they doing. Noa was exactly the opposite of me; there was not one thing in our hobbies, friends, looks, tastes, and personalities that we shared, and yet it worked great, both then and today. Noa is still one of my dearest friends. My life was like no one else's; as a teen, I learned to adjust my passions to my life, schedule, and surroundings. I was a reader and was called every name in the book: bookworm, nerd, apple, et cetera. I was proud of all those names. I loved to read and no name-calling could take it away from me. I also loved classical music, which did not always go along with my friends' musical tastes in the youth house. Listening to Tchaikovsky helped me to calm down when I felt rattled. Most teens made fun of that too, but I still listened to him. I did great among my friends when Queen was playing at full volume from my cassette player that once in a while would skip. Yes, I also loved rock music.

I enjoyed being with my peers and yet would give myself a time out, especially on the days they were looking for adventure. To me, they were just looking for trouble and I had enough on my plate. I never felt that I needed to get into trouble to get attention from our keepers. Somehow I would be in trouble once in a while, whether I liked it or not, and I could not figure out why. I sure can now. For instance, one day I did not feel well so I stayed in my room and did not go to school. My keeper, Ron T., arrived at our room after he saw that I was absent at breakfast. Noa told him that I was not well.

"I will ask Rosa to check on you," he said.

Rosa was our housekeeper, mother, friend, and

often a comforting ear.

"Ron said,You will stay in your room and I will see you at lunch. I hope you feel better."

Then, Ron walked out of the room. After lunch, I felt much better. I told Roni but he insisted that I stay in my room and rest. Roni checked in on me in the afternoon and I was not in my room. So what if he said to stay? I was feeling good and went to help in the chicken coop to immunize the chickens and transport them. We were studying five long days and working one day a week. Saturday was a day off unless it was our turn to work. We had a cycle of every few weeks to work on Saturday.

My working place was the chicken coop. I knew they were working extra hours to finish transporting the chickens, so all I wanted to do was to help; no harm done, or so I thought. Roni K. was part of the team and spotted me on the tractor with the chickens. Etzik, the man in charge of the chickens and also a supervisor, was driving it and I was sitting next to a volunteer that I liked. My problem was that my team knew it: he was in his late 20's and I was a teen. We were driving to the other group to exchange the chickens.

Roni K said, "Get off the tractor, young lady. Have a shower. I will see soon." He did not look or sound happy.

"The tractor is going down. I will get off then."

"Off now!"

You see what I mean? I wanted to do a good thing, and I now had a big problem. I did not need to sneak alcohol or cigarettes into the room to see all of my keepers with frowning faces.

Our youth group, much like any other group, had the dominant leaders, the subservient followers, and the loners. A few of us, myself included, were everyone's friend. That is, until one of the alpha girls decided to bully another girl. I asked the girl who was being bullied to let me help her, but she declined my offer. Eventually, something happened and I could no longer stay on the sidelines and watch. Late one night, the bully cracked eggs on my roommate our first year in the kibbutz. I woke up to her screaming and was shocked when I saw her. She had stinky, dried eggs all over her hair, pillow and blanket. I asked her if she knew who did it, and she replied that she had one suspect in mind. We called our guardians and I tried to calm her down and comfort her as much as I could. While she had a shower and our guardians had an emergency meeting, I changed her sheets.

The guardians decided to blame one of the boys and said, "If it is not him the person who did it should come forward," and left it up to us hoping the guilty party would come forward. When I overheard the female bully bragging about what she did to her loyal followers, I snuck out of my bedroom window and went to Sarah to tell her the truth. The boy they claimed did it was not involved at all—for a change.

Sarah said, "I am taking your words to the guardians meeting today."

I went back to our room and told the group that I will speak the truth even if they think I am a tattletale. This is reprehensible behavior and I will not sit back and tolerate it while someone is abusing one of us. That day I became one of the most hated people on the kibbutz. I was very sad about this because people knew what I did was right and they did nothing about it, just like they did nothing about the bully.

That evening, I opened the door to go to the meeting and most of the group was waiting there for me. When I stepped out of my room, they all spit on me. I walked back in to change my saliva-soaked clothes, then walked right back out and said, "I dare you to do that again." Thankfully, no one did.

In our meeting, the guardians said, "If no one comes forward all of you will be punished and the boy who we think did it will stay to work this weekend." I was furious, and had no plans to leave with a later bus to Eilat. It is a long journey by bus, and to start it at noon means I won't be home until the early evening, besides the fact that I refused to be punished for something that I did not do. I stood up and said to the bully girl, "I have no plans on being punished because of you. You are only a hero in the dark. Why won't you take responsibility for your actions?"

With those few comments, I was able to end bullying for good on the kibbutz.

After that ordeal, I was not the most popular girl, but I think I earned the most respect, which in my opinion is much better.

I was seventeen when my future husband started courting me. He was nice and gentle but I had no interest in him. I had had enough of the males. They never grew up. I learned this by getting hurt by a young man I dated. We were together for more than a year; he was in the kibbutz part of the Nahal program. When this young man moved out to the base, he decided that two girls were better than one. When I found out, I helped him make his deception easy by telling him,

"With me, it is only one. In this case, it is not me."

Then I dated a volunteer, supposedly an adult, who was about twenty-four years old. All he wanted to do was to get drunk and take me to bed. Needless to say, he did not last long.

To his credit, my first husband was persistent and never gave up, even though every time he wanted to be alone with me, I refused. I did not know him and had no ambition to learn who he was. One evening after dinner, we were all outside the dining room chatting, and somehow they all left, one by one, until there were only three of us remaining. When Stephen said, "I'll leave you two, good night." I knew that that was the plan.

My new boyfriend asked me to go with him for a walk to the stables. Well, someone had done his homework. I liked that a lot. His quiet voice and British accent were intriguing.

We were dating when my sister Iris and my Mother saw us together for the first time. They knew we would get married; they saw something I did not, but they were right.

Most evenings I spent studying for my high school finals in his room. It was quite relaxing and far from the hectic life I had in the youth house. His bachelor room turned out to be clean and tidy within days of the first time I stepped into it. I'm not sure if he liked it but he did not complain. He liked to walk into the room after long day of work and see me there, half asleep on my notebooks.

"Take a break," he would say.

By the time hc would return from the shower, I was ready to leave.

In Israel, at the age of eighteen, you can drink alcohol. I was done with high school and preparing for military duty. During this period, I worked full time and had no time for social life except on the weekends. When high school was over, we moved out of the youth house and lived with partners in a bigger room in a different area. We were all going to be soldiers. At first, Noa and I decided to stay roommates, this time in a little complex where we each had a room but shared a bathroom and entry. We knew each other's weak and strong points and were comfortable with each other. I did not take into consideration that my boyfriend status had changed. He was no longer a volunteer. He wanted to stay in the kibbutz so he went to the Olpan. I spent more nights with him than with Noa, so we decided to be roommates. We moved together into a two-room complex. He worked with the cows and I worked in the field from morning to evening, went to the stables for an hour or so, and got back home late at night. We had a great life together when we saw each other, which was very little. Shortly after I started military duty, my boyfriend brought a puppy home. She was adorable, like every puppy. He named her Kim. We also had an old cat who adopted us; his name was Koki, and he was Kim's protector. Even though she quickly grew bigger than he was, she still had a lot of respect for her big "brother."

I would split my military weekend vacations between my parents in Eilat and my boyfriend on the kibbutz. At first, it was an even split and then it was more boyfriend than parents. I knew that he was my future: we were a "family" already, living together, with pets. When he asked me to marry him, I did not hesitate, and with all my heart I wanted to have a family and be with him, forever.

On the eighth month of my first pregnancy, I was dreaming of my son. I called my mother; she was in the United States with my sister Iris and brother Arye.

I said, "I have a boy: he looks just like his Dad, tiny nose, brown eyes, lush lips, round face." I gave my Mom the exact details of the boy I was dreaming of.

Mom was holding her breath, "Did you give birth?" She asked, knowing that I did not want to know the baby's gender until I gave birth.

"No." I said. "I was dreaming of him."

Two weeks later, on September 14th, she was back in Israel, and I gave birth a perfect baby boy. He looked exactly like he had in my dream. If I had not called my mother to tell her about my dream, no one would have believed me.

At first, I wanted to call our baby boy Yam, which translates from Hebrew to "sea" because of my passion and love of the sea. My husband was British and said, "We cannot call him Yam; it is a vegetable in England." Now that I live in the United States, I am so glad I did not name my son after a root vegetable. Think of all the trouble he would have suffered from his classmates at school!

Right after giving birth, our baby boy was wide awake, with eyes open, clean white skin, almost smiling. He looked so calm and did not cry; he reminded me of the soft flow of a river. We named our baby boy Yarden, translated from Hebrew to Jordan. Today, Yarden is a young adult and he looks exactly like his father. Yarden's English birth date, September 14th, had no meaning at his time of birth.

I was in week 38 and his time came. His Hebrew date was very important, as it was Kippur eve, what a date! Yarden was in my arms before noon, then at 13:00 (1:00 PM), my husband and Mom left me until the following night when Kippur was over and they could drive again. I had the nursery crew all to myself; no one wants a baby on Kippur eve. The positive aspect of that situation is that they let Yarden stay with me all day. Before I left home, I had the opportunity to bathe him, change his diapers, and nurse him. He was so small it felt safe doing it in the hospital with the nurses beside me.

I remember one of the times I was breast-feeding Yarden, I talked to him and said, "There must be something special about today." I felt like the only new mother in all of Israel that had no visitors, flowers, or chocolate.

Yarden was a beautiful baby and very easy. I could not understand parents that did not sleep at night or complained that their baby cried a lot and was restless and challenging. Yarden was so good that I thought I would have lots of children, and planned a second child. It did not take me long: the day I said to my husband that I wanted a second child is the day I conceived. Only 838 days after Yarden's birth, I gave birth to Shani, my punishment for being so arrogant.

Shani cried from day three until she was four months old—straight, nonstop. Maybe she had a problem with digestion, the doctor said. He couldn't find anything medically wrong with her. I only breast-fed her, so I changed my diet. She knew what she wanted; I, on the other hand, had a hard time reading her mind. After some time, I learned that she did not like a wet diaper; not even a drop in it. No wonder she was potty trained at eighteen months. I had to catch her hunger three minutes exactly before she asked for it, or else. She liked to be on her belly, reach forward with her hand for a toy that was just the right distance so she could stretch. After four months of this nightmare, my thoughts of having many children were gone.

All Shani wanted was to be mobile. At four months and one day, Shani became the girl we know today—the most charming, easy, loving, mobile child. She had a private clock: at six months, the doctor checked her and asked, "Can she reach an object when she sees it in front of her? Can she lift her chest while on her belly?"

I looked at him and said, "She is crawling faster than me and she is standing."

"What else can she do? The doctor asked"

"She has been sitting on her own since she was four and a half months, sitting at the table, drinking from a baby cup, and eating independently." I replied.

"What about her behavior? Is she still crying? "

"No, Doctor. She has not cried since the day she started crawling."

Even though it was only four rough months, the thought of having more children did not return for another six years.

We became accustomed to routine family life: two children, home, dog, and work. We did not have a healthy marriage life, but it could have been worse. We were arguing. I did the talking, he watched TV, and off we went to bed, a little frustrated—but we had two beautiful, charming, smart, healthy babies, and for that I was grateful.

In 1996, I worked with the youth, closing a cycle perhaps. Zohar G. was in charge and I helped him. Later when Zohar changed positions, I learned his responsibilities and took over his positions as a consultant. There was a group of German youths that were being hosted in Maale Hachamisha's hotel, where they learned about history, culture, and religion. They asked to team up with the youth in the kibbutz and we did; it was a great experience for both groups. We were thinking of going to visit them in Germany. This was still in the planning process and needed a push from the German side. We explained to them that the budget for such a trip was beyond our ability, and they helped us out. Two years of hard work—physical and mental—were about to pay off. As an extra adult, I was looking for a parent to travel with me. It was overwhelming to travel with 16 sixteen-year-olds to Germany all by myself. Shalom S. volunteered and this worked out to our advantage, as Shalom speaks and understandsthe German language, besides the fact that he was a superb help for me.

"Dad?" I said, a little worried, "I will be traveling to Germany with the youth and wanted to tell you that we will be next to Hamburg. Is there anything you would like me to bring, do, or buy?"

"Not really, but if you can find my brother Arye's grave, it would be good."

It was the very first time I had heard about an Uncle named Arye. I could not wait to get to my father. I was expecting a logical explanation.

Searching for Fred

Chapter 3

The Drive To The Truth

The drive to my father's house usually takes about four hours. I like to take a break in the middle of the three-hundred-and-fifty kilometer stretch; it is not long but with a ninety kilometer an hour limit, it sure does feel that way. My favorite view is the desert, the silhouettes of the mountains, carved out by flowing water, animal tracks in the sandy dirt, and Acacias punctuating both sides of the road. Driving in the Aravah prairie is relaxing and often a succession of images, thoughts, sounds, and emotions pass through my mind.

This particular drive sent my brain into overdrive: did I ever hear the name Arye as my father's brother? All I remembered was that Dad had once said that he came from Hamburg.

No one talked about the Second World War: it was a forbidden subject. There was no memory of talking about the past—our lives started the day we were born. We are the family and the beginning of a tree. I never heard stories about Grandfather Karl.

"All you need to know is that his name was Karl," Dad said when I asked him about my grandfather.

Grandmother Elizabeth passed away when I was two years old; I have no memory of her, either. My aunts did everything in their power to leave the war behind them, without much success I might add. Filled with curiosity, I wondered what was so important that Dad wanted me to drive all the way to Eilat and that he could not tell me over the phone.

Finally, I arrived. As soon as I walked through the door, I noticed a bottle of vodka sitting on the table.

"Dad, are you feeling well?" I asked.

"Sit! Do not worry, I did not start yet. I was waiting for you." Dad said.

I smiled. "You know I do not drink hard liquor. Is there any beer in the refrigerator?" I asked with some relief and some worry, realizing that my father himself thought this was going to be a difficult spill.

"Well then," I said, "it looks like we are going to have a party. I will fix something to eat. You cannot drink this bottle with no food; you are too heavy to carry."

Dad came to the kitchen and asked me why I had left the kibbutz an hour earlier than I previously said I would. He had expected me to arrive around three o'clock. I told him I had not left early. I had left at eleven just like I said I would.

"Nava, it is only two. How could you be here? How fast did you drive?"

I chuckled: it is not like me to speed. I knew that road very well and my knowledge of where every police car sits and at what time was incredible.

"It is a very dangerous road. You should be very careful; there are a lot of maniacs driving, especially on the prairie stretch, it is like a jungle out there."

"Fine, Dad. I will be very careful."

We set our little private party with Dad's favorite herring, chopped salad, black bread, olives, and home made pickles.

Nervous and ready, I said, "Tell me. I am all ears."

If predicting the future were in my power, I would have known to bring a tape recorder. After a few minutes, when Dad was going on like a machine —talking so fast it sounded like he was being chased and needed to get it all out before he was caught.

I said, "Please stop."

I asked him to take a deep breath. I searched for a pen and paper in the bedroom, and found a drawer of old documents that almost looked like Dad had been looking for something but could not find it. Dad was very neat, and leaving the drawer this way was not like him.

"Ready again, can you start from the beginning? Please go slower so I can make sense of your words."

It was the longest conversation I ever had with my father. My ears stretched up in the air like they did not believe what they were hearing, and my eyes were wide open like it was the very first time they saw the man in front of them.

"His name is Arye," Dad began. "We were in a youth house in Blankenese, Hamburg. Just before we immigrated to Israel, Arye drowned in the pool."

It was the second time in my life that I saw my father cry; the first was when he held Yarden at his circumcision and was announced as the Godfather for my firstborn.

"Arye Leckner in Hamburg cemetery should not be that difficult," I said.

"How come you never mentioned Arye before?"

"No need to dig in the past," he said. "Now that I know you will be nearby, it would be nice if you could go to the grave, if it is there, and if it is possible to find it at all. Fifty years is a long time to be alone with no one to pray for you."

My father stunned me with his words. He never believed in God, or so I thought. He respected our religious neighbors, we celebrated all the holidays, but he never kept any of the mitzvahs. He continued.

"Before we immigrated to Palestine, they split the children by age group: Grandmother Elizabeth and my three sisters, Rina, Tami, and Lea, stayed together. Aunt Roti was alone. I came at a different time on the Providence. We found each other well after we all arrived."

"How was it in the war?" I asked.

My father looked like he was living the time again; his eyes opened wide, with a scared look in them. "Hungry," he said. "We were hungry for years, because I was the oldest. Six years old, and it was my responsibility to sneak out at night to search for leftover food and bring it home. Bread crusts and potato skins were my target, but anything edible would do." Suddenly, I understood why my father stored food for "just in case"; he was living alone and had cupboards of preserves and a freezer stuffed to the top with meat. He did not want to go hungry ever again.

"Remember, your aunts were babies, so they received the food first, then Arye, then Roti. I was last because I was the oldest at the time."

It was not easy for me to recap my Dad's route to becoming a survivor. He had so many blanks on the map. Dad was born in Danzig (Free City). Today it is Gdansk, Poland. Around 1945 they had to leave Danzig because the situation got worse, and as a mixed family (my Grandfather was a Catholic

German solider) they were able to quietly leave the city without anyone bothering them. No one helped them, but they left them alone. When the war intensified, more Germans occupied the city. Then, the mixed families were forced out of the city, only to arrive in Berlin and then move into hiding on Amrum Island. We don't know who moved them or why. When the war was over, someone from the island sent signals saying there were survivors on the island. My family were rescued and taken to Hamburg, Germany. Although we could recognize Dad, Karl Jr. and Roti on the Blankenese photos there is no record of them in writing.

Dad was on his way to Israel on the illegal refugee ship "Providence," departing on May 10, 1948 from Marseille, France. At sea they heard of the Declaration of Independence of Israel by Ben Gurion. At sea their status changed to legal and became a immigrant ship "Providence." On May 22nd, Dad disembarked the ship without the status of refugee and would not go to British detention camps in Cyprus. As a legal immigrant, he immediately joined the Palmach and fought for his country. So many blanks to fill and still a lot of questions unanswered.

I called my Aunt Roti, wanting to find out more information regarding Uncle Arye.

"Are you out of your mind?" She said. "There is no brother Arye. It is all your father's imagination. He is not thinking right. Stop digging in the past."

Dad said there was an Arye; Aunt Roti said there was no Arye. Nevertheless, I was traveling to Hamburg and I had nothing to lose.

In Hamburg, I was a guest of the Horst family. The day we gave our youth a day off to be with their host families, Brigit and I hit the train looking for Arye's grave. Hamburg has two Jewish cemeteries. Of course, we had to go to the wrong one first. By the time we visited the second one it was closed. My hopes were that tomorrow when we returned we would have someone to talk to, perhaps get some help, too.

In 1998, the cemetery used the original notebooks from 1947, where they kept the records of the dead. I asked the gentleman for Arye Leckner who had passed away in 1946 or 1947 at maybe eight or nine years old. My hands were shaky, my heart pounded, and my thoughts raced out of control. Is it really possible that I have an Uncle Arye here? It was almost like fighting a dream, one of those dreams that you want to end and are anxious to finish.

"Here," he said, "Karl Leckner, nine years old, nineteen-forty-something." He had a hard time reading the numbers and refused to let us look.

"Karl" I said and went silent. Of course, this must be the name on his birth certificate, the name Arye must have come later. They probably gave them Hebrew names before they immigrated to Palestine, just like Dad and my Aunt; that was it.

"My Grandfather's name is Karl Leckner. I am sure this is it. Can we see him now?" I asked. I could not wait to go out of that room and march to my uncle, to tell him about his survivor sisters and brother.

The gentleman was holding a long stick. He pointed it to the wall and said, "It is here."

I looked at Brigit, puzzled. "Can you ask him for a map?" I asked her.

"No maps; try to remember the wall map," he said.

We both fixed our eyes on the wall map to try to commit it to memory. We marched to the area that we remembered, and looked for my uncle for more than an hour. The old part of the cemetery was jungle-like; some graves had trees growing right out of them, splitting the graves in half. Some of the sections were under a heavy bushy area that was not possible to reach. If my uncle's grave was among those graves, we would not be able to see it. With no luck, a little frustrated, we went back to the office to ask for help.

"I am not helping; I am busy," he said.

I saw his sour face; it was unfortunate that he could not speak English so I could tell him what I thought of him. I looked at Brigit. "I know you do not have to be here, spending your day off in the cemetery, but do you mind if we search for it again?"

"I do not mind," she replied to me.

I smiled and thanked her as we went back to the search. We knew we were in the right area but could not find it. Like an angel coming to our rescue, the gentleman appeared with a group of people. What do you know? He was helping them to find their loved ones: a group of Americans. I went to the man who looked to be in charge and explained the situation to him. I asked him if we could join the group. He looked at the cemetery keeper with hard eyes, then asked us to join them and commanded the keeper to tell us where Karl was when we got there.

We made it! I looked at Karl's grave; it was bare, with only a little bit of gravel and some scattered wood that could have dropped in from anywhere and fallen onto it. No wonder we could not find it; there was no mark, name, or sign, so there was nothing to recognize. Looking carefully, with tears running down my cheeks, I saw what looked like something written on the pieces of wood. My love for puzzles paid off.

With patience, I gathered together the wood and it said, "Karl Leckner, something 2, 10." Later we learned that those numbers are the grave mark, section line and the number of the grave. My heart was pounding. I was so excited and shaky it was difficult for me to light the candle and say a prayer. Brigit did not know what to do, looking at me, filled with emotion. She asked to help with the matches to light the candle, but I politely refused. It was something I needed to do, for Dad and for myself.

Just before we left Karl Leckner Jr., I looked down on the wood and said, "One day, I will be back with a real stone, Uncle Karl."

The little plank that they had placed on the gravel in 1947 was still there, in very small pieces, fifty years later, waiting for me to find it—it was nearly impossible to comprehend.

I came back home with photos from Karl's grave. My father was beside himself.

"You did it!" He said. "I should have known that you would!"

I explained to Dad in the smallest details how we found the grave. He asked over and over again how I did it, his "stubborn girl."

Mission accomplished, I thought, but I did not have the chance to hold onto that thought for long.

"Nava," Dad said, "there are more."

"More what?"

"More siblings."

"Where?"

"In England."

Here we go again. I learned from the first time that the smallest detail could be the most important one. I wrote down every single word Dad said. After Dad finished telling me the story, I asked some questions, but to most, Dad did not have an answer. I wanted to organize the information he had just given me so that I would have a timeline in chronological order.

"I have a brother named Fred and a sister named Gerda. I think Gerda is older, but I am not sure. They are both older than me, and their last name is not Leckner; my birth name is not Leckner. I cannot remember the name—Grandma gave me Leckner because she was married to Karl and he raised me. All of your aunts in Israel are Leckners. Karl was a German soldier. I have another figure in my mind but I do not know who he is. He was an officer for sure. His boots were tall and shiny and made of leather, like riding boots. The uniform he was wearing was so tight pressed it could stand up by itself, and it looked like even his hat was pressed. I don't think my birthday is my actual birthday, but I don't know what it is.

Loewenthal is a name that I remember, but I am not sure about that either. It could be Mayerson or Aharonson, too. I think one of these names were my grandparents. Gerda and Fred were transported to England at the beginning of the war with lots of other kids. Your grandmother knew where they were, but burned all records. She said Fred is a British soldier and he did not want any contact with us. Later, I learned from Uncle Fred that this was completely false. We never got in touch, and all my life I was dreaming about finding them. You found Karl; do you think you can find Fred and Gerda?" Overwhelmed with my new discovery, I could not think of searching for anyone. "You are not a Leckner? I am not Leckner?" I asked my Dad.

"I do not think I am. I was a little boy, but I know Karl came into my life and not me into his life. If you can find my name, maybe you can find Gerda and Fred."

"How can I find anything?" I asked.

"You want me to find a needle in a haystack— Gerda and Fred in the entire United Kingdom! Are you serious? What if she got married? What if he immigrated to some other country?"

With Gerda and Fred's information still in my mind Dad said, "One more thing, while I am telling you all of this you should know that there is one more baby that I remember on Amrum Island but can't remember anything about him and he did not immigrate with Grandma and your aunts."

When I saw my father's despair, I promised him to do my very best to find Gerda and Fred. I called my Aunt again and told her that I had found Karl's grave in Hamburg Germany and that Dad had asked me to look for Gerda and Fred.

"Why are you doing it?" she asked. "Leave the past; tell your father to stop dreaming. They are not coming back."

I had caught her! "So you say that there is a Gerda and a Fred?"

She chuckled. "Yes, somewhere in the world."

The conversation with my Aunt Roti cheered me a little. Although she did not show signs of happiness, something in her voice was not as negative as the first time I talked to her and asked about Arye—I should say, Karl Jr. I told Roti that Dad said that Karl Jr. drowned in some pool.

She replied, "I do not think so. He was sick and even though he survived the war, he could not recover."

I now had two theories. Maybe one day I would know the true reason. "Aunt Roti, would you like a photo of Karl Jr.'s Grave?" I asked.

"Yes," she replied blankly.

It seemed to me that the looking was difficult for my aunt, not the finding.

Chapter 4

Falling Apart

Living in the kibbutz was good for raising the children, having the comfort of close friends and being surrounded with support, but I still have to say that the system was not the best fit for my needs and life at that particular time. My family was outside the kibbutz; they all lived in the cities. Mom and Dad were in Eilat, and they were both sick. Mom had a long battle with cancer and Dad's overall health was declining, so the distance between us was very difficult. I had my life; work, two toddlers, and a marriage that was falling apart. Overwhelmed with responsibilities and life duties, I felt at times that something had to change.

The first thing was our marriage: it could not continue the way it was. I felt miserable and trapped. My attempts to talk to my husband regarding our communication, raising children, household responsibilities, and sex life were failing. He knew the importance of family to me, and that gave him the confidence that I would never leave him.

I said to him, "One day you will lose me."

His response was to turn on the television. As insulting as it was, I continued carrying on with our life—together, yet apart. Mom started her long recovery from cancer, but the worries and frustration from the fact that I was so far from her and could not help as much as I wanted did not help me mentally. Dad's condition worsened and he moved to Haifa, near my older sisters, thinking that would be better for him and there was a better hospital for dialysis treatment. We knew that Dad was living on borrowed time but we had no idea that his time was so short. Yarden was four years old and Shani two years old. I had my hands full.

With guilt on my shoulders, I found myself in a stranger's arms—a lover. It was no angelic act. I knew it was wrong and had no excuse for my bad behavior, but I did not want to stop the affair. I felt loved again, more like a human and less like a robot. I knew it would have to stop, one way or another. I just did not want it to stop then.

In all of the confusion and turmoil in my life, Dad's condition became worse than ever; it was the end. I knew it and did not want to believe it. I used to drive to visit Dad in Eilat every time he called— we called it "night shifts." Finish working at about four o'clock, pick up the kids from kindergarten, make sure they are clean and fed, and then call the person who was in charge of the car arrangements. In the kibbutz, we had no ownership of property; we shared everything including the cars. Most of the time, night drives to Eilat were not a problem. I could leave at about six or seven in the evening to get to Eilat at night, clean Dad's house, and make us something to eat. If he was in the hospital, I would visit him there for few hours and then drive back home to start a new day. I returned with enough time for a shower, prepare the kids for school, and go to work. Weekends and days were more of a problem. I did not always have the opportunity to get a car and if I did, it wasn't for a long enough time, as I needed ten hours for a round trip. To top it off, we had to pay for it from a small budget, which made it a challenging situation.

Six months before Dad passed away, he moved to Haifa, thinking that getting close to the center of the country will be better for him. My older sister lived in Haifa and the rest of us, except Ofer who was in Eilat, were closer to him. Most definitely that move made it easier to reach Dad. I could take the bus to Haifa and didn't need to depend on the availability of the kibbutz cars.

Dad was dying. I finally came to that realization and really wanted to be ready for it. What I discovered is that nothing can prepare you for the loss of a parent. I visited Haifa as often as I could. Two weeks before the end, I called Mom and told her that if she would like to see Dad ever again, she should come to visit as soon as possible. She did. Dad loved Mom until the very end. He always regretted that they had gotten a divorce and always said that she was the best. Every time Mom had a boyfriend, Dad would find some defects about him. He was funny in this matter: even the way the man had their hair was not good. I remember asking Dad to give the man a break, and thank god he can breathe. Dad looked at me and said, "If it were up to me, he would not breathe."

I laughed so hard that day.

My first husband, Mom, Yarden, Shani, and I drove to visit Grandpa Yuval. The kids loved him, especially Yarden. They had a strong bond; it was well known that Yarden was Dad's favorite grandson. It was hard to see Dad sitting in a wheelchair, wrapped with bandages from the feet to the knee, and they were soaking wet.

"Grandpa," said Yarden.

"Yes?" Dad answered back.

"Does it hurt? Your legs? Can you walk?"

"Do not worry, Yarden. Grandpa will be fine," he answered.

My heart broke when I saw tears in Dad's eyes. He knew he was not going to be fine, but how can you tell your five-year-old grandson that you are dying? Dad left it for us to do, so we went to Dad's house to eat lunch, but really to give Mom and Dad a chance to say good-bye. At the end of the visit, we kissed and hugged. With broken hearts, sadness and silence, we drove back to the kibbutz. For my husband, Mom, Yarden, and Shani, it was the last time to see father. I was with him as often as I could be. The two hour drive to visit Dad were easy and short compared to the trip to Eilat, and for that I was grateful. Dad and I would talk on the phone every day, sometimes twice a day. The last day, I called early in the morning, before I went to work. The nurse said that Dad had had a long night and he was in dialysis treatment. I left a message with her and told her I would call later. I did as I said but the nurse still would not let me talk to him. She said he was tired and to try later. The second time, I was very concerned and I called my sister. Unfortunately, she confirmed my bad vibes. After talking to the family all night long, the first thing in the morning—

5:00 AM to be exact—I found my way to Haifa. Dad was in bed, in and out of consciousness. When he was conscious, he looked around but did not seem to know where he was. His arm was in the air, his head looking in the same direction as his arm, and he repeated the same sentence over and over again, arm waving: "Go away, go away!" Arm reaching, "Mama, Mama!"

My heart was breaking. My father, the strong man I had known all my life was having a horrible end of life. I was very frustrated because there was nothing I could do to ease his pain and discomfort. This was the end, and there was nothing anyone could do about it.

While all three of his daughters were there to witness this, the two sons were away.

"I am coming now," Ofer said. "I need to bring Dad a photo of Osher." Osher was Ofers first-born child.

"Don't be silly," I told him. "If you leave now, you will get here late at night anyway. Stay with your wife and newborn. Come on the first morning bus to Haifa; you will be here by noon."

We were waiting for the neurologist to visit Dad. None of the medical staff members showed any concern that Dad would pass away that day. We all believed that Ofer and Elan had more time.

The unthinkable happened: I had to leave Dad and return the car to the kibbutz. I called Meir, the kibbutz's car manager, and asked him to let me stay with Dad, as he was in critical condition, but Meir said he couldn't because the car was assigned to someone else and I had to get it back right away.

I looked at my sisters and said, "If Dad comes out of his delusional state, you tell him I was here all day for him and that I will be back as soon as I can." I looked at the clock and said, "He should see the doctor any minute. In five hours, I will see you again. Hopefully, we will have the results of the last test."

I hugged my sisters and left with a heavy heart. I called my sisters every fifteen minutes. I wanted to hear good news and talk to Dad, but I had no luck. I drove to the kibbutz, dropped off the car very angry and agitated, and made sure Meir knew it. I was polite and respectful but with a very strong message. Going back to Haifa was a long two hours. I had to return via public transportation; first the bus to Jerusalem from the kibbutz, then a second bus to Tel Aviv and at last the train to Haifa. It is not difficult or uncomfortable on a normal day, but when you know it could be your father's last day on earth, every time I made a transfer I felt like crying. It was an excruciatingly long trip.

My last call before I arrived at the hospital was from the train, "Ofra, give me good news. I am almost there."

"Dad is up. Talk to him." She said.

"Nava, where are you?" Dad said.

"I was there with you all day. I had to return the car to the kibbutz. I will see you in ten minutes," I said, but he didn't answer.

Ofra was on the phone. "He's out again."

"Did you tell him I was there?"

"Yes we did."

Those words were my last exchange with my Dad. I found out that the doctor did not attend to him all day. I decided to find him and physically bring him to Dad. By the time I tracked him down, he was at my Dad's side. I had followed the doctor from one station to the other. Just as I got to Dad's room, the nurse brought the crash cart in and closed the door on me.

I called Mom and said, "It's the end, the crash cart just went in, don't tell Ofer yet until I talk to the doctor."

A few minutes later the doctor came out.

Shoshan Purim will never be the same. I called Mom again and confirmed the sad news, made sure she emphasized to Ofer that even if he would leave Eilat when he planed to, he would never make it on time. I had no time to mourn as I stayed behind to take care of the formalities for the funeral. I had to do all the paper work and fly with Dad to Eilat. My sisters and their families drove to Eilat the same evening. I finally fell asleep on a chair outside of the morgue, still in disbelief that my father was gone. After the Shiva, one week later, I was back at the kibbutz with Yarden, Shani, my husband, and my lover. I made up my mind had to get my life back together. Everything was falling apart around me.

Dad's house in Eilat was ours; we had bought it many years prior to Dad's death and he had lived there mortgage and rent free. I decided to leave the kibbutz and move into the city. My husband agreed, saying that maybe if we changed our way of living our relationship would get better. I have to admit that I loved it in the little house in Eilat, to be back next to the Red Sea, surrounded by desert and hugged by the sun most days of the year. I loved it.

I had to part from my lover, and I did all I could to build our family life again.

Everything fell back into place except the relationship with my husband. I went to college while the kids were in school, and had an after-school program at home so that I could be with Yarden and Shani. Financially, we were good. The kids were happy. We fixed up Dad's house to perfection.

I couldn't live without love and intimacy. I felt too young to have such a routine. I was only twenty-seven. Old people lived like that, not me! (That thought would come back to bite me later.) And yet,

I didn't want anything to do with men. Everywhere I went there were predators. My college professor, at the grocery store and the pharmacy, the father of one of my students—they all took on the shape of a praying mantis.

A few months after the move to Eilat, my cousin Arye called me. "I need your help in two days," he said.

"I have a new opportunity for business in Eilat, but the gentlemen will not come unless I have forty people in the audience. You are going to be one of the forty."

"I have no interest in a new business, nor do I have the time," I answered

"Just come and help," he pleaded.

I was there to help set up the room, and that's when I met Tom Chernoff. The meeting was a success, I thought to myself. Even though I heard nothing of what was said by Tom, I was intrigued by the man who stood in front of me. I just smiled at him and felt that he was talking to me only.

After the meeting, Arye, his wife, Tom, Efi, and I went to the promenade to have a drink. After relaxing from business to a more casual and comfortable zone, Tom asked more private questions. I volunteered very little information back. How could I tell a complete stranger that my marriage was a disaster? We had such a good time that evening that we decided to get together for breakfast. Tom and Efi flew back to Tel Aviv. We parted with an exchange of phone numbers.

The following day, Tom and I exchanged some e mails regarding the business, as he needed help with translating documents. I enjoyed Tom's personality so it truly started as a working relationship. A few months into the business—and not to my cousin's liking—Tom and I became more than just business associates.

"I cannot do it," I told Tom, when it felt like we were going to be involved romantically. "I did it before. It is not fair to my husband and the children. I may not be happy or satisfied, but I am a married woman."

A little frustrated, Tom respected me, and the situation. Trying to cool things between us, we made hours for work so that there would be more focus on that and less on us. This did not work at all—we could not be apart. I was married with two young children, and Tom was also married. His wife stayed in the United States when he came to Israel with his business. We had to arrive at a solution. In-between was not an option for me: it was all or nothing.

At that time, I went home after a visit to Tel Aviv and asked my husband to join me on the couch because I needed to talk to him. The kids were asleep, and I had lots on my mind and in my heart.

"I want a divorce," I said. "I am moving to the United States to be with Tom, and I am taking the kids with me."

"You must be on your period," he replied. "I will talk to you in few days."

Most of our conversations did not go well; why should this one be different?

"I am not on my hormonal cycle now, and I am leaving you. I hope you understand." I replied

It was very hard to do. I never intended to get a divorce; I wanted the marriage to last forever and ever, but we had grown apart so much that it could never work. On the day of the divorce, I cried my eyes out.

"Why are you crying?" He asked. "You wanted this."

"I am truly sorry. When we got married, I wanted it to be a fairy tale, but we can't build a bridge over the space between us and you know it."

I got on the bus back to Eilat to be with the kids, while he went to Tel Aviv to be with his friends. Most of my family and close friends did not approve of my actions. Everyone thought my husband was the "perfect" guy, and Tom was the exact opposite, in their eyes. Tom was older, much older. When we met, he was sixty-nine years old, older than my Mom but younger than my Dad (or so we thought until I found out when my Dad's birthday actually was).

There were forty years between us and that was the only thing they could see. I was worried more about the kids than about Tom's age and wondered why no one bothered to ask if he was capable of taking care of two young ones and me.

"Age means nothing if you are happy," I said repeatedly.

"You are crazy! You are going to be a young widow with two children in a strange country," my sister claimed.

None of their concern mattered to me. I had made up my mind. The only person who could stop me was Tom himself and he had no intention of doing so. I finally told them all to support me or to leave me alone. I'd made up my mind to be with Tom, and that, as they say, was that.

"I am doing it. We want to be together. I am not a baby, and I am more than capable of taking care of my family if things go wrong. If I'm destined to be a young widow that had only a few good years of marriage, it is better than a lifetime of misery."

That was my last statement to my mom before we moved. I could not have been happier for us all: not to give anyone the wrong impression that it was easy. The divorce, family disputes, and the move to America were all very difficult and challenging, but this was the best thing I could do for me, and my children. Tom and I started from nothing; we had given everything we had to our exes, just so we would have no fights with them. Seventy years old and thirty years old, with five- and seven-year-old children, we were starting a new life in a new country.

I had to stop the search for my uncle and aunt for few

months because of all the changes in my life, but soon after the move, I was back on it. Tom saw my determination and said, "I know you will find them. I will be here to witness it, too," even during the times when it seemed impossible.

Chapter 5

The Search

Back Side of the Prayer Book

When the search for my Aunt Gerda and Uncle Fred began, computers were not my forte and search engines were not as effective as they are today. Most of my search for the first few years was by snail mail. The fact of the matter was that I had no clue how to look for Aunt Gerda and Uncle Fred.

The starting point was very frustrating, since the search began with few to no details regarding their location, last names, families or even ages. I did not have any ideas or the right tools, so I started with searching for Aunt Gerda and Uncle Fred in England. This was a big mistake—huge—and it cost me years of searching with nothing to show for it. It is comparable to searching for someone named Joe in New York City: like finding a needle in a haystack.

When I had my Dad cooperating with me, I learned that it is better to start the search from the end and not from the beginning. Going back as far as I could and following my father's footsteps was the better way, even just for the reason of starting to learn the family whereabouts and escape during the war. Before Dad passed away, he would read any new evidence I uncovered. Sometimes it would jostle his memory and help with the family history or whereabouts. After Dad passed away, I had to work with new material by myself.

The young adults of the community in Danzig had been transported to England on the "Kinder Transport." I finally hit useful information! I stumbled upon the Kinder Transport by accident, so I thought that was a step in the right direction. Now elated and sure that the search was close to an end, I found an organization that had all the details regarding the transport, including names and dates. So, I sent them a letter asking for information regarding my aunt and uncle, licked the stamp, which suddenly tasted great, and with a shaking hand I sent the letter.

Just to remind you, the letter had to fly to England, be reviewed, and with approval, I would get a wonderful answer. This was only in my best dreams, but giving up is not in my nature. I checked the mailbox every day twice a day for months, hoping that I would have a reply, only to learn that the AJR organization, due to their privacy policy, could not tell me where Aunt Gerda and Uncle Fred were. I could not prove to them that Uncle Fred was my uncle and that Aunt Gerda was my aunt. I was not immediate family to them and I needed consent. Consent? If I had consent from Fred or Gerda, I would have no need for the search! So how could I prove that my father is Gerda and Fred's brother? I could not. After several exchanges with AJR, I gave up on them and looked for different venue. It was sad to learn that they could help but chose not to, without going into details and understanding the policy of privacy and the right of the people. My clock was ticking. We were talking of second and third generations of survivors.

Here is the biggest problem that I had: The man that I call my father—Yuval Leckner—who was born March 1, 1932, is really Eitel Loewenthal, who was born on November 23, 1932. Even if my own life depended on it, I could not prove that these two were the same person. It is so complicated to explain that most people just say, "You are not who you say you are," without learning the details. Just before the immigration of my family to Palestine, they had their names changed to Hebrew names. On top of that, they changed my father's birthday so that he could fight for Palestine. None of the children had any documents of proof. Dad said that one day they walked by and told them that from now on they had Hebrew names and this is how Eitel became Yuval.

Some of the letters that I sent with requests for information were more like throwing darts at a target in a dark room, but I had nothing to lose, as my frustration grew bigger and felt that I was running out of time. I knew that Gerda and Fred were older, and Dad was in his late sixties, which made them in their seventies and maybe in poor health or worse. I was very sorry that I was right regarding one of them: Aunt Gerda had already passed away. One of my shot-in-the-dark letters was to a Gdansk archive. I have to say that I was surprised to see a response a few months later, as my letter to them was very confusing, even for me. I told them I was searching for Gerda and Fred who maybe had the last name Leckner, Meyersohn, Aharonson, or Loewenthal, and I wasn't sure if I was spelling the names right. They replied to me on December 2, 2005:

Dear Madam,

In response to your enquiry, I have to inform you that we have found only a confirmation of the fact that your family lived in Gdansk, which has been found in the "Neue Adressbuch in Danzig" ("The Addressbook in Gdansk").

For Example:
—in 1928, Lewenthal Rosa, Ruth, Herbert and Amalie lived at 24 Abtsmuhle Street;
—in 1931, Rosa, Ruth, Herbert lived at the same address.
Leckner —the family name—is not mentioned in this publication, in which 1941 is the last year mentioned there.

We are putting your request forward to the State Registry in Gdansk. The money you have given we will treat as a deposit and we are going to spend it for the service searching the above mentioned Registry.

Furthermore, we suggest contacting the Jewish Registry in New York. To the best of my knowledge, the Registry of the Gdansk Jewish Community was transferred there as early as 1939. Additionally, we recommend books on the Jewish Community in Gdansk by the Polish authors, Abramowicz and Domanska (unfortunately, I do not know if there are English translations).

Thank you for contacting our library. We hope that the results of our research helped you.

Yours faithfully,

Beata XXXXXXX

Information Science

Biblioteka Gdanska PAN

Saying that they would search for the information that I sent them made me feel so good. Finally, someone cared. I was ecstatic. I doubt the woman who replied to my letter understood the impact of this. I don't know if she was just doing her job or was on it just to help out. I do know that this woman made it all possible for me, and renewed my energy to continue my search and the finding of my uncle and aunt.

I GOT IT! Gdansk archives did it! They found my uncle and aunt in the old records. Fred Loewenthal, born September 14, 1939. Gerda Loewenthal, born October 6, 1928. I had real names, with proper spellings, and birth dates. These were sure things for finding them—real, authentic records. I wrote the archive back and asked for records for the rest of the family on behalf of my aunts, and they all received their birth records. What great people work in the archives in Gdansk, Poland. The one record they could not find was my father's.

During my research, I stumbled over a web site that held my surviving family's records, which indicated that my father's name was Leckner, so my search was for Leckner and not Loewenthal for some time. It all of a sudden clicked in my mind, why my son's birthday was when it was. My son, Yarden, and Uncle Fred share the same birthday, sixty-three years apart. That date seemed to be very important in my search, as I had every clue under my nose without knowing it. This would all become clear soon.

Shushan Purim—March 2, 1999—was a very tragic day in my life. My dear father passed away, and the last words he spoke to me were, "Nava, where are you?"

Dad passed away, but I did not stop searching. Internet databases improved, and more details regarding the Second World War were exposed. This is how I learned about the list.

Contacting someone who responded was great. When you feel so close and so positive, it is like climbing to the top of the world. Then comes the fall that is worse than the one that was before. I believe it was Dr. Peter who sent me a copy of the cards that they had in their possession. In fact, this card confirmed that my father's name was Eitel but, to my surprise, I learned that he was registered in Israel as nine months older than he actually was. When Dad had once told me once that he thought he was younger than the birth date on his driver's license, I had not absorbed it. It was an insignificant detail in my opinion, but later proved that every little detail has significance.

I was one step closer to finding Gerda and Fred. I had confirmed that they were on the Kinder Transport and I had everyone's original names. The processing of every detail was taking months and years, and my clock was still ticking. Gerda and Fred were older than my Dad. Gerda's record from 1947 stated that Gerda Loewenthal was now Taylor. Because Fred's record did not have any change of name, I assumed he was still Loewenthal. This was another big mistake, and this one cost me two years.

Gerda's name was changed because her family adopted her, so she became Taylor. Fred's name was also Taylor, but never officially, so his record stayed Loewenthal. Looking for Gerda did not help due to the fact that she remarried and her last name was Abrams. Two long years went by with absolutely nothing as far as my original search, but I did find a cousin in Germany. While talking to the family about my research, I found out that a cousin of mine, Roni, who was also searching for our family, so from one we became two and we helped and shared the information we had. Andrea and Yuachim in Germany, very friendly cousins, were also a big help. After cross checking the information we had, we found out that our grandmothers were sisters. They were looking for Lotty, my grandmother's sister.

Sometimes the information I carried with me was good but hurt the research. Helping Andrea and Yuachim taught me another lesson—to cross-reference my knowledge with others. In Yad Vashem, I found a document about Lotty that indicated that she had been in the Stutthof concentration camp. With the document in my hand, I visited the archives of Stutthof concentration camp —only to find that there were no records indicating that Lotty was ever there. The worst part of research is that after years of building a theory, it comes crashing down around you and you need to go back to the beginning. Do not ever give up: if you do not find a grave, there is still hope. Unfortunately, a lot of our subjects were murdered and vanished into thin air.

As my research and knowledge grew, I learned more about other families, history, and survivors. I always have respect for those who share their horror stories with the world, even though they know that the world cannot comprehend it. It is not easy to stand up publicly and announce that your family was shot in front of your eyes, but you lived because the Nazi officer liked you and used you for sex; that you begged for him to kill you when he was done with his brutal act; and that you are still standing to tell the story. Or, another survival story of a woman who gave birth to a beautiful baby boy: the Nazis let her breast-feed the baby for two days when she had enough milk they tied her breast and monitored how long it would take for her or the baby to die. She said she had to kill her baby boy. He was dying from starvation, and to take her own life meant to kill him too by another brutal experience. Listening to these awful stories, I understood my fortune: my Dad had survived and as result of it, I was born.

Searching for Fred

Chapter 6

The Time Is Right

First Hug

There is a reason for everything in life, and my ten years of searching had finally come to an end. My cousin called to say that she had found Gerda's daughter. By the time that was one hundred percent confirmed, I had also received a letter from England stating that Uncle Fred was located.

Four weeks after the visit with Uncle Fred, Ofer found Jeanne, Gerda's daughter. Was it the right time? Probably. After ten years of searching, we found Uncle Fred three times in one month. I could not stop smiling at the immense thrill of finding Uncle Fred and my cousins. I called my husband at the office,

"Tom, we are flying to England!" I said, before he could say hello on the phone.

"When are we flying and why?"

"To see Uncle Fred," I said casually, and then I screamed into the phone, "We are going to Uncle Fred—Uncle Fred in England!"

Two weeks after the end of the search Uncle Fred, Tom and I were in the airport on our way to British soil. When Tom gave me the boarding pass, he said, "Here you go my little firecracker."

I had big smile, sparkling eyes, and disbelief all at once. I could swear that if I were to walk the streets of England and see this man walking towards me, I would know exactly who he was, as my Uncle Fred looked exactly like my father. I would later learn that they shared a very similar personality. Later that day Ofer landed in England. His response was the same as mine.

"They look the same," Ofer said.

At five-foot-five, Uncle Fred is little taller than Dad, but they have the same green eyes and the same "worker" hands. As Uncle Fred says "Not the hands of a concert pianist." They sit, walk and even curse the same way. We met Gerda's daughters and grandchildren that weekend, along with Uncle Fred's close friends and neighbors. Tom, Ofer and I felt like part of the family, as if we were never separated for all these years. It was just so natural, and I finally understood the true meaning of the phrase "blood is thicker then water."

While it was a joyous occasion and a happy reunion, sadness permeated the occasion due to the fact that my father was not present to see his big brother. And also for Fred, for his life was filled with abuse and terror. The Kinder Transport was, for the most part, a good solution for the children. However, as I learned, my uncle was in the horrific minority, where verbal and physical abuse were an everyday part of his childhood life.

Tom and I flew back home, with the face of my uncle engraved in my brain. His hands felt just like my Dad's. It had been a long ten years; a weekend visit in England was not enough. Tom hugged me and as if reading my mind and said,

"You will see him again soon. I will make sure of it."

So, on the way back home, I had nine hours to create a family reunion between Uncle Fred and all of his sisters: Roti, Tami, Rina, Lea, and all of his nephews and nieces, and all of his grand nephews and grand nieces, among them Yarden and Shani.

I did it—all nine hours I was plotting and planning, my mind circling.

On June 2006, my uncle Fred flew to Israel from England. We flew to Israel from Pittsburgh, and for the first time ever, all of the siblings were together. I tried to organize our family tree and documents into an easy-to-read book with everything that I had collected throughout the years, including birth certificates for all of us. Each one received a custom-made book to show how we were related. Later in the evening, when we sat together, relaxed and with dry eyes, we all opened the books and I guided them all to show how they were related to all of my findings. It was not an easy task, as two out of the four did not know that they did not share the same father as my Dad. In addition, they were so confused regarding Karl Jr. and what had happened to him.

"There are still many unanswered questions that we most likely will never know." I told my aunts.

"I cannot answer everything, and some questions I don't want to answer. I am happy that this family is back together, and more so because I made it happen."

Tami was hurt by one of Dad's continuous comments. They were very close.

"He always said we are all from a different milk man, but I never thought he was serious about it," she told us.

What about me? I can't prove that Dad is my biological father: a baby boy was born in Danzig on November 23, 1932, as Eitel Loewenthal, and the same baby boy buried in Eilat, Israel, as Yuval

Leckner. His grave says that he was born on March 1, 1932, and nothing in between exists as far as documents for a change of name. One day, my grandmother woke up, said he is a Leckner, and Leckner he became.

Aunt Rina said, "Yuval always said that we are from different milkmen, but this slut from a good Jewish home needed help not only from the milkman but also from the butcher and the baker to have nine babies while the man in her life is dying."

The room burst with laughter. After lunch, hugging and crying, to close the circle we all went to the cemetery to say a prayer next to my grandmother and father's graves. Uncle Fred had someone holding his hand at all times; it was almost a unity of worry. He was crying, shaking, laughing, and sweating. It was a lot to comprehend for all of us.

By the end of the day, we all felt like we had never been apart and the sixty-seven years were bridged very quickly. The scars that the war had left on each one of them can never truly be mended, but for one day I gave them some closure and happy moments. We were so wired that night we could not go to sleep. Tom grabbed his cigars while I opened a bottle of red wine and sat outside. All of a sudden, they all joined us; apparently, no one was able to sleep. That is, until Uncle Fred started to snooze and snore. "Uncle Fred, it was a busy, exciting, and exhausting day. Why don't you go to sleep?" I asked.

"I am not asleep," he replied.

"That is exactly what Dad would say," Ofra, Ofer, and I said at the same time. We laughed so hard, just letting it all out. The following day we showed Uncle Fred where Dad had lived, toured the city, and went to a very special place to eat. We warned Uncle Fred that it was not a traditional restaurant but good earthy food. He agreed to go.

"Most definitely a different way of eating," said my British uncle, as he ate—with his hands—pita, hummus, and Labane at Yosoph's tent.

Searching for Fred

Chapter 7

Closure

In the summer of 2009, I was able to fulfill my promise to Karl Jr. We went back to his grave in Germany with a beautiful headstone that I had made in Pittsburgh, Pennsylvania by Urbach Memorials. Their team was so kind and helpful, as we had very unusual request. "This headstone will fly to Europe, then will cross the country by car, will visit Poland, and finally will get to its destination in Hamburg, Germany, so please make it beautiful, but small, not too heavy, but sturdy, preferably under one hundred pounds so we can carry it and not send it with the luggage." They did just that. Perfect!

Uncle Fred, Tom, Yarden, Shani, and I experienced a very special trip to Germany and Poland; we followed most of my father's Holocaust survival route including Blankenese, Germany, and a visit with Dr. Martin. We saw the house that Uncle Fred and Dad had lived in and two more apartments the family had lived in before they were forced out of Danzig, known today as beautiful Gdansk. Part of my discovery was where they lived and with whom. Following the old address book and map and comparing it to the new Gdansk map, we found all three houses. We had two days in Gdansk and lots to do. We walked all day long. The family agreed that we could not call this trip a vacation because on a vacation you are supposed to gain weight, not lose it. It was the first time we met my cousin Andrea, her husband, and their beautiful family.

On my birthday in May, Uncle Fred had called me and said, "I didn't send a gift because I want to give it to you on the trip."

I didn't think much of it, said thank you, and closed the subject. At the end of the last day in Gdansk, Uncle Fred came down to the dining room with a wrapped gift and said, "I know you are the person to treasure it the most. Happy birthday, Nava."

I opened it and could not believe my eyes. When we had visited Uncle Fred for the first time in England, he told me that the only thing he had from his past was a prayer book, and he showed it to us.

A few years ago, he had it restored. My hands were shaking as I held it.

"There are dates on it," I said to Tom. "You will never believe it if I tell you. Look at it!"

Tom did, and for the first time, he was speechless. I have always believed that dates are meaningful; sometimes we just don't know why. In this case, I knew it a little too late, but I was still surprised by it. Glued on the inside of the prayer book on the first page was Uncle Fred's photograph as a child and Uncle Fred's birth date; September 14, 1931. On the last page was the date of the Kinder Transport leaving Danzig May 3rd 1939. For my entire research of many years I had had clues right in front of me for how to find my uncle that I did not know it until after I found him. Yarden, my son, was born on September 14th, and my birthday is May 3rd.

"This prayer book has survived so much. It deserves a lot of respect and care," I said to Uncle Fred, and thanked him for sharing it with me. That prayer book was my birthday gift; I received it in the same city it had left seventy years earlier. The day before we had to fly back to the states, we visited Uncle Karl Jr.'s grave with our very special headstone. Rabbi Shlomo Bistritzky from Chabad, Hamburg was so kind to join us at the cemetery to say the prayer. It was so satisfying to be there with the family and Uncle Fred.

I looked at the headstone, looked at Tom, and said, "We did it."

It was closure for a very long journey, complete with the ups and downs. I am forever grateful for having the opportunity to meet so many wonderful people who are dealing with such a dark history.

Now, Uncle Fred visits us every year for several months at a time. We take great pleasure in having him around. From the moment we met, we felt like close family and everything that comes with that.

Uncle Fred still learning the Jewish holidays and some traditions that he is not accustomed to.

When our son Yarden did Aliyah to the Torah at the age of thirteen—Bar Mitzvah—Rabbi Ely Rosenfeld from the Chabad center in Fox Chapel made sure that Uncle Fred, at the age of seventy six, would have his Aliyah to the Torah, too.

On Tom's 80th birthday, Uncle Fred said that he never believed he would live to be that old. Uncle Fred is only six weeks younger than Tom.

"Speak for yourself; I am not old," said Tom.

"Remember what Mom Alice said. Age is only a mental stage," I added.

My wonderful and much appreciated mother in-law is ninety-eight years old, very independent, and claims, "I still have all my marbles."

I want to believe that with his new life Uncle Fred will be around for many more years—he has seventy years to catch up with. My Timothy (or Tom, as everyone else calls him) is young at heart, and we are celebrating our tenth wedding anniversary on October 2012 and very much looking forward to our silver anniversary.

Uncle Fred recounted to me, "The only memory I have of your Dad is playing next to the river bank, and we saw a body floating down the river. I cannot remember him or how he looks, but I remember being with my little brother. I don't have a lot of memories from the past; only a few, and I hold onto them with my dear life because that is all I had when the Taylors' told me that my entire family died in the war, that I am no longer Jewish, and I am going to learn a new religion.

"I also remember a man, a striking and smart man with polished boots and ironed uniforms. I understand that Yuval described the same man. It is possible that this one is our father, but we will never know. As you know, all three of us were given our Mother's maiden name of Loewenthal. I also remember someone was born and someone died; I am not sure in what order or how, but the cause of the situation stuck in my mind. Mother is shouting for help in the one bedroom we lived in with a few children and a few adults. One of the adults made a curtain so we would not see her, but the shouting... one cannot forget that, and then a baby's cry. It could have been Roti, it could have been Karl Jr.

"One night was especially quiet. I remember someone on the floor covered with blanket. To my question of "What happened?" I received a reply, "He's dead," and again, my dear Nava, I cannot remember how it was. My last memory from Danzig...I remember getting a small bag and being pushed onto a train. That turned out to be the Kinder Transport.

"In England, I remember being taking to the Taylor's, but Gerda did not come with me. I was told I would see her later. I fell asleep. In the morning, I woke up to a smell that I never dreamed of, it was so good on the nose, and I was happy. They asked me to come to the table, and I was introduced to bacon and eggs. It was delicious; I had never had such a big breakfast in my life. It was like a meal for the whole week. Later that day, I was given banana. I started to eat it with the skin, and I didn't like it at all. When the Taylors saw this, they showed me how to eat the banana, and other fruits and vegetables.

"My very first Christmas, I was so surprised at all the festive feelings, the good food, and lots of presents. I felt really good, but this 'honeymoon' lasted only a few months. Gerda had her family; they adopted her. She did well in school, and was very happy. As for me, everything was exactly the opposite. I did poorly in school–now, I know I am dyslexic, but back then they didn't know what that was so they treated me like I was mentally retarded. I got into trouble in school, and when I went home, if Mr. Taylor had talked to the teacher, I knew I was in a big trouble. He would beat me all over my body. I was in pain for days. So that people would not notice, he mostly avoided my face. One time, he beat me on my face and I was forced to wear a ski mask so that no one would see. At times, it was so bad that I thought I was going to die.

"At fourteen, I quit school and went to work. I had to earn my living in the Taylors' house, and I gave my entire income to them. At sixteen, I left home. I couldn't bear it anymore and I was big enough to do so. My relationship with Gerda drifted apart; I felt like she didn't want me in her life. She never said anything or did anything to prove my feelings correct; it was just the way things were. When Ruth and I got married, I finally thought that my life was going the right way: a loving wife, house, work—a man's dream—but that was not the case at all. Shortly after our wedding, Ruth got sick, very sick, and dependent on me. When she felt a little better, we wished for a child, and she got pregnant. That day was such a happy day! And again a trauma happened. Ruth had a miscarriage. After that, her health, mentally and physically, was poor. She never got pregnant again, and then she passed away from cancer. "

"Here I am, at the age of eighty, looking up and I see my new beautiful god-sent family. I wish I had known your Dad and all my sisters years ago. I never saw Yuval after the Kinder Transport and I am very sorry for that, but he left you behind to find me. With you, Tom, Yarden, Shani and all of your brothers and sisters, I am blessed with a new family and a new life."

Searching for Fred

Epilogue

No Regrets

I always feel that it is necessary to work together with the people in my life, whether it's with my partner, co-workers, or friends and family. As individuals, we need to fulfill our dreams and goals, and to make that happen we often rely on those we know for help. You should never give up on something important to you because as long as you're still breathing, it is not too late to achieve your goals. Sometimes we might have delays—life is full of surprises—but quitting completely is never a good option. Without our dreams, who are we?

When I started my search for Uncle Fred and Aunt Gerda, it seemed like an impossible task. At times I felt like a hamster on a wheel, running and running and getting nowhere. Was I wasting my time? Time I could have spent with my family, instead of chasing after rainbows. Pushing the growing "SEARCH" folder aside did not help my restless brain stop thinking of the whereabouts my uncle and aunt. The longer it took for me to find them the more I worried that maybe they are no longer living. Every single day made a difference in the search.

"Maybe Dad will see Uncle Fred again," is one of the thoughts and regrets that never leave me. My father and Uncle Fred were not able to meet again. We were so close and yet so far. But if I gave up I would never have met my Uncle and all the cousins that live around the world. Our children would never know their true family tree. It is true that there are still many questions left unanswered, such as, "Who is my Grandfather?" However, there are more that were answered. I made a lot of people happy by not giving up my search when it was leading nowhere. Uncle Fred lived an enormous lie most of his life thinking that his entire family were exterminated in the war, but now he has the truth and some answers. We cannot rewind the time but it is possible to give the past a new meaning. I am thankful for having the opportunity of making so many people at peace with their unmistakably horrifying past.

If you are a person who is searching for someone, do not give up. You just might find your long lost family. If I hurt anyone on my way to finding my family, my apologies, but I have to admit that if it was part of the search and brought me closer to what was destined, I have no regrets. Never live your life saying, "I should have." If you want to do something that is significant to you, just do it.

I would like to give special thanks to the survivors who were willing to share their stories so that the past will never be forgotten. Their life mission is that we all stand together regardless of gender, race, religion or disability and to make sure these atrocities will never happen again.

Don't forget but PLEASE forgive.

PEACE, LOVE AND HAPPINESS TO ALL

Timeline

&

Documents

Timeline

Name	Event	Date	Place
Karl August Leckner	Born	July 21, 1896	
Elizabeth (Grandma) Loewenthal	Born	July 20, 1911	Strassburg
Gerda Loewenthal	Born	October 6, 1928	Danzig, Free City
Fred Paul Loewenthal	Born	September 14, 1931	Danzig, Free City
Eitel (Dad) Loewenthal	Born	November 23, 1932	Danzig, Free City
Elizabeth & Karl Sr.	Married	October 20, 1936	Danzig, Free City
Helga Leckner	Born	January 21, 1937	Danzig, Free City
Karl August Jr.	Born	July 15, 1938	Danzig, Free City
Fred & Gerda Loewenthal	Kindertransport	May 3, 1939	Danzig to England
Karin Leckner	Born	February 11, 1940	Danzig, Free City
Gudrun Leckner	Born	September 5, 1941	Danzig, Free City
Karl Sr.	Died	January 19, 1943	died in line of duty (WW2) in Latvia

144

Leckner Clan	Rescued from Amrum Island and transferred to Bergen-Belsen and Blankenese	1945
Eitel (Dad)	**Change name to Yuval. Started his journey to Israel as Yuval Leckner, born March 1, 1931**	**1946 Hamburg, Germany**
Karl Jr.	Died 1946	Hamburg, Germany
Elizabeth & the babies	**Given Hebrew names and immigrated to Israel**	**Hamburg, Germany**
Eitel (Dad)	Arrived to Israel on the ship Providence	May 22, 1948
Elizabeth	**remarried to Mr. Steinberg**	**Eilat, Israel**
Nava Leckner	Born May 3, 1972	Eilat, Israel
Elizabeth	**Died. April 7, 1974 Grave stone says "Aliza (Leckner) Steinberg**	**Eilat, Israel**
Gerda	Died 1977	Bolton, England
Nava & first husband	**Married**	**June 1993 Maale Hachamisha, Israel**
Yarden (son)	Born September 14, 1994	Jerusalem, Israel
Shani (daughter)	**Born December 30, 1996**	**Jerusalem, Israel**

| Nava & Yuval | Learning about the family history for the first time. | 1997 | Eilat, Israel |

Karl Jr. Grave found in **October 1998** **Hamburg, Germany**

| Yuval (dad) | Died | March 2, 1999 | Haifa, Israel |

Nava & first husband Divorced **November 26, 2001** **Beer Sheva, Israel**

| Nava, Yarden & Shani | Moved to USA | December 10, 2001 | Coral Springs, Fl, USA |

Nava & Tom **Married** **October 21, 2002** **Fort Lauderdale, Fl, USA**

| Uncle Fred | Found | May 2006 | Nether Kellet, England |

Fred, Tom, Ofer and Nava **Met for the first time** **June 16, 2006** **Manchester, England**

| The Family | Family Reunion | July 16, 2006 | Eilat, Israel |

Uncle Fred & Yarden **Bar-Mitzvah** **October 2007** **Fox Chapel, PA USA**

| Karl Jr. | New Grave stone | July 15, 2009 (His birthday) | Hamburg, Germany |

THE SAME MAN

Birth Certificate

Family Name: Loewenthal
First Name: Eitel Yoachim
Father's First Name: None
Mother's First Name: Elisabeth
Date of Birth: November 23, 1932

Death Certificate

Family Name: Leckner
First Name: Yuval
Father's First Name: Karl
Mother's First Name: Elisabeth
Date of Birth: March 1, 1932

Copy
From Lt.Col.Eric Warburg   A. P.W. I D.
      H.Q.   A.O.O   696

                                    June 17th, 1945

To
Military Government
Hamburg, Germany

My family and myself have been approached by the American
Joint Distribution Committee with regard to the property
at Hamburg -----HAMBURG KOESTERBERG -----and have asked me
if I was prepared to put this property temporarily at the
disposal of the American Joint Distribution Committee to
house and shleter such Jews who have returned from Nazi
concentration camps.

I understand that the estate is at the present time being
used as a German Military Hospital, but that arrangements
are being made to evacuate it. Naturally, I do not want to
make suggestions to the Military Government of how to make
use of the estate under the present circumstances. However,
the purpose of these lines, which the representative of the
Joint Distribution Committee is taking with him to present
to you, is merely to tell you that the American Joint
Distribution Committee's plan to use the estate for the
purpose of those unfortunate ones who are now returning
from Concentration camps is one which I and my family are
in complete sympathy with, and we would welcome it.

                         Respectfully yours
)signed) Erich M.WARBURG
                         Lt. Col. A.C.   A.U.S.

Grandmother Elizabeth wanted Fred and Gerda back as soon as the war was over, but unfortunately she never got her wish. Fred's foster family lied to him and told him that his entire family was killed in the war. Grandmother also asked that Fred be raised Jewish, but the foster family did not let a Rabbi see or talk to him.

```
14.8:46.  From Mrs. Hardisty acknowledging receipt of copy of letter
          we sent to Fred's mother.
14.5.46.  To Mrs. Hardisty giving her details of Miss Cohen's letter,
          and telling her it is being put forward at the Religious
          Committee Meeting to-morrow.  Also asking her to discuss
          it with Lord Gorell and let us know what he feels about
          the matter.
16.5.46.  To Miss Cohen asking her to get Fred's mother to send a
          signed statement to us similar to the one that she made
          on her behalf, as we feel sure no action can be taken
          without it.
22.5.46.  From Mrs. Hardisty enclosing translated copy of Mrs. Pomera's
          letter, to us sent to Fred's mother, asking her to sign a
          letter saying she wished Fred to be moved.
22.5.46.  To Mrs.Hardisty, we have written asking Miss Cohen to get
          Fred's mother to sign a statement similar to that one made
          on her behalf, so we did not think it will be necessary in
          the circumstances to send the translation.
26.5.46.  From Miss Cohen, Mrs. L. very upset but will not let herself
          say she has heard from Fred himself.
1.... .   To Mrs. Hardisty - We could let Fred go to...
... .     translation to Miss Cohen for transmission to Mrs. L.
11... .   Letter to Mrs. Hardisty enclosing ... for...
1.11.46.  To Miss Cohen, will she ask Mrs. Lowenthal to let us have
          some kind of statement, as we cannot do anything in Fred's
          case unless we have a direct statement. Also to find out
          whether Mrs. Lowenthal has heard from Fred or his sister.
11.11.46. Letter from Miss Cohen, Relief Worker, enclosing copy of
          letter Gerda sent to her mother which makes it obvious that
          Mrs. Lowenthal has given the children permission to decide
          their own religious future.
1.11.46.  To Mrs Hardisty sending copy of Gerda's letter.
14.11.46. Letter to Miss Cohen acknowledging hers.
18.11.46. From Mrs. Hardisty Have we ever had letter from Mrs. L.
20.11.46. To Mrs. Hardisty. No.
```

http://www.uni-heidelberg.de/institute/sonst/aj/INSTITUT/BERLIN1/
l.htm

Central archives for the study of the history of the Jews in
Germany:
Existence: Institutions: Jewish municipality to Berlin: DP card
index
Listing of the persons

L

Surname, First Name, Date of Birth, Place of Birth, Number on the Map

Leckner, Eitel, 23,11,32, Danzig, 8032
Leckner, Elizabeth, 20,07,11, Strasbourg, 8033
Leckner, Gudrun, 05,09,41, Danzig, 8034
Leckner, Helga, 21,01,37, Danzig, 8035
Leckner, Karin, 11,02,40, Danzig, 8036
Leckner, Karl, 15,07,38, Danzig, 8037
Leckner, Liselotte, 12,02,43, Danzig

Front Side of the Prayer Book

Anläßlich der Auswanderung aus Danzig
mit dem ersten Kindertransport nach
England als Erinnerungsgabe überreicht
vom
Vorstand der Synagogengemeinde
zu Danzig

Danzig, den 3. Mai 1939

Translation:
In connection with emigration from Gdansk
with the first Kindertransport to
England as a souvenir gift
presented by
the community synagogue Vorstand
in Gdansk
Gdansk, 3 May 1939

Dad in front of the "White House" gate

Uncle Karl on the "White House" grounds, second
from the top

The "White House" with all the tenants, Dad in the bottom row seventh from the left, with the dog:

Sinai 1973

Sinai 1976

Me as a Sergeant in the Israeli Army with my dog, 1992

Karl Jr.'s Grave as I found it in 1998:

Karl Jr.'s new grave stone:

Uncle Fred with all of his sisters by their Mother's grave (2006)

Uncle Fred with his nephew Ofer

First kiss with Uncle Fred's great-niece

Uncle Fred with his nieces

Uncle Fred wis his Great - nephew and Great - nieces

Gdansk (Danzig) 2009

Aunt Gerda, Uncle Fred and Dad were born here:

Second house

Bar-Mitzvah Boys, Ages 76 and 13, 2007

Aunt Gerda

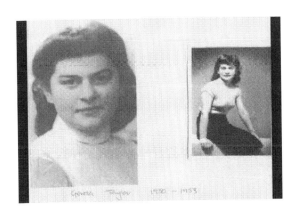

Uncle Fred   Dad

Dear Reader,

I know you have many titles and authors to choose from and I appreciate you choosing my memoir. As a token of my gratitude, I would like to offer you a personalized bookmark free of charge. Please visit my website for details:

www.navachernoff.com

Until next time...

Best Wishes,

Nava Chernoff

Searching for Fred

Searching for Fred

Made in the USA
Charleston, SC
11 November 2012